There Is A CRACK In My Pot

There Is A
CRACK
In My Pot

PATRICIA ANN FORBES

XULON PRESS

Xulon Press
2301 Lucien Way #415
Maitland, FL 32751
407.339.4217
www.xulonpress.com

Printed in the United States of America.

ISBN-13: 978-1-54565-337-1

TABLE OF CONTENTS

ACKNOWLEDGMENT

First and foremost, without Jesus, I am nothing. Thank you, Father, for speaking to my heart to write this book. I thank you, Father, that I heard Your voice and obeyed.

Father, you are truly amazing, and You are a God that never lies. I am totally amazed at You, and I love You with all my heart, mind, soul, and strength.

DEDICATION

I **dedicate this book to: my children, Ralph, La'Tisha,** and La'Shauna; my awesome husband, Rodwell; my grandchildren, Angela, Josiah, Jeremiah, Shamond, Jada, Layla, Brandi, Amana, Isaiah, and Serenity; my brothers, William, Charles, and Curtis, and my one sister, Sharonda. I dedicate this also to all my aunts, uncles, cousins, nieces, and nephews.

The Situation
There's a CRACK *in My Pot*

INTRODUCTION

We moved around often when I was growing up. I would often remember so many details about the moves. At one point, the house we lived in was only one bedroom, and my mom made her living room into a bedroom. We had bunk beds for my two brothers and me; I slept on the top bunk, and my two brothers slept together on the bottom bunk bed. Our dad was a truck driver, so most of the time we only saw him on the weekends. When my dad was home, he and my mom couldn't tolerate each other and the home would be in an uproar.

My mom worked very hard to keep the family together, no matter what the situations were like. She would work two jobs, the two positions that I remember the most were her jobs as a housekeeper for families living in the upper-class neighborhood, "across the tracks" what we call it in my hometown, and a housekeeper at Holiday Inn.

Mom worked seven days a week—Monday through Friday in the private homes and Saturday and Sunday at the Holiday Inn. My older brother was responsible for taking care of my younger brothers and me while Mom was at work.

Even with all the days my mom was working, there still was not enough income for our family. During these years, we received government assistance. I will never forget the government cheese truck that came to our neighborhood once a week, delivering commodity goods to the low-income families. We all looked forward to the cheese, because this cheese made the best cheese sandwiches. Some of you who are reading this know what I am talking about; and as a matter of fact, you want one of those sandwiches right now.

My mother and her dad played significant roles in our lives. Granddad lived in the next town, which was about thirty minutes from the city we lived in at the time. We saw him on a regular basis; he would bring us food and often give my mother money to help take care of us.

When my dad was in town, he spent quality time with my older brother and me. On Sundays, my dad would take my brother and me to the baseball game. The baseball game was the hang-out for most of the locals in my town after Sunday morning church. My mom did not go to the baseball game with us; to this day, I don't know the reason why. Well, my brother and I enjoyed the game, eating the hot dogs and peanuts and drinking that good old Nehi grape soda.

The comments from the people overwhelmed us; they often told my dad about how beautiful we were. Of course, we were trained to say thank you, no matter how many times we got commented.

Because of the not-so-good relationship my mom and dad had, my dad eventually moved to Philadelphia, Pennsylvania. Mom eventually went to Philadelphia, and while she was there, my brothers and me stayed with my aunt. Within a couple of months, we all were packing up to relocate with my dad, where we spent about half a year in Philadelphia.

My dad was not light on the bottle (alcohol), and my mom could not take the pressure of living in a problematic relationship with my dad any longer. My dad's job was during the night hours, and sometimes on the weekends, and my mom's job was doing housekeeping at the Marriott Hotel in downtown Philadelphia. She told us that she was going to save her money to move, and within a month we would move back to Florida.

She kept her word. We all traveled back to Florida on the Greyhound bus. In other words, it was like we did a disappearing act on my dad.

At the time, my baby brother was only a year-and-a-half-old. Mom made his bottles and made us cold-cut sandwiches, along with peanut butter-and-jelly sandwiches, with lots of fruit and water. We traveled for about two days back to her hometown of Madison, Florida. My mom's sister met us at the Greyhound bus station to pick us up. So now, here we go again, returning to Florida.

As a young child, I didn't know if this was good or bad, but at one point I was glad to return home to Florida, because the school I attended in Philadelphia was much different than the school I had attended in Florida. There was this girl who bullied me daily.

Once we returned to Florida, I remember the house we moved into so well. It was a two-bedroom with an outdoor toilet—not an outhouse because this toilet flushed. We all had to take our baths in a tin tub. My mom would make the hot water on the stove and mix it with cold water for us to take a bath. I remember this one time; I poured the hot water on my younger brother and myself, and of course, Mom had to take me to the hospital due to my screaming and crying about the water burning my foot; I would not stop crying. I was showing off to get my mom's attention, but I came to find out my brother was burned more than me.

I also remember, while staying in this house, that there was a creek behind the house. Mom would tell us, "Don't go to the stream." One morning, during the summer months when Florida would have the most rain, when we woke up, the creek had risen; the water from the stream had come up to our porch.

Every day before she would leave the house for work, Mom would say, "Don't go to the creek." So one day, when she had gone to her friend's house, a couple of my friends and myself went back to the stream, and on the way back to the house, I got a stick stuck in my leg. I had disobeyed, and now I was in trouble. Mom had to take me to the hospital to get the stick removed and, let me tell you, I still have the scar on my leg to this day.

We didn't live in this house for a long time but during the time we did, when the seasons changed, and the leaves fell, Mom would have us rake the yard. Our house was close to the road; the front porch was about fifty meters from the road. This one time, we had raked the yard and piled the leaves close to the road. So, on this particular day, my baby brother and I were playing, jumping on the leaves, and not paying attention to whether a car was coming or not. But before I knew it, there was a car, and my little brother got hit by the vehicle. It was an unfortunate day.

My mom was in the house and because of my screaming, she came running to the door. I will never forget this day. My mom was wearing white shorts that were covered with the blood from my brother's ear, which was popped loose from the car rolling over his head three times: one time forward, then the vehicle backed up and ran over him again. By me screaming, the vehicle went forward over my brother's head once again. The car finally stopped, and the taxi driver rushed my mom and brother to the hospital. Thank God my brother only has a a couple stitches from his ear popped loose. The blood I saw on my mom freaked me out though.

I believe this was a hard thing for my mom, it changed everything in our home. My brother had many doctor visits. My mom often spoke words to my brother that change him and the way he saw the world. My mom would say negative words to my brother. You are crazy and stupid. Shortly after this incident, we moved to another house that was only a couple of feet larger than the one we were staying in before. The difference was the bathroom was in the house, with a bathtub. We all were excited! It reminded me of *The Jeffersons* (we're moving on up). I was still sharing the bedroom with my brothers. Within one year, we were moving again.

The small town where I lived decided to build a project neighborhood. My mother was praying for us to get an apartment in the project. Yes, I was excited about this because I would be able to have a room to myself. I don't know about other projects around the world, but this one was based on your income, and yes, we qualified.

Mom never believed in leaving anyone behind, so she shared the information with her best friend. She made sure they would stay close together. When moving time came, they were next-door neighbors. You know how duplexes are; they lived that close to each other.

Things changed again in our lives, as I could see the vision my mom had for us was coming to life. It was as if God had lifted a significant burden off of my mom.

My granddad would still visit us often and would take my brothers and me to visit with him over the weekend. During these visits, we would spend Sundays in church all day. My granddad was a man of God and made sure his grandchildren were in the house of the Lord. I remember trying to understand about God at that young age; it was hard for me because my comprehension was feeble. I didn't realize this until my school years.

MY SCHOOL YEARS

I noticed at a young age that something was missing, and I was not like all the other children. There was a missing link, and I knew it had something to do with my learning ability.

My spelling, reading, and speaking were off. There were many areas of learning I could not understand and words I could not pronounce or spell. Around the third grade, I realized my inability to comprehend. In my mind, I thought I was like any other child, but I soon came to realize I was not.

In my third-grade year, I had the opportunity to have my mother's sister as my class substitute teacher for a week. My aunt was a very educated lady and accepted nothing but the best in my learning. However, she soon found out that my reading, spelling, and speaking abilities were not up to my grade level. In my class, there were different levels of reading groups; the reading levels were intermediate through advance. My reading group was the intermediate (slow) reading group in my class.

In the slower-reading group I tried hard to read, but there were still words I could not pronounce. The harder I tried, the more I failed. I would sit silently and would not look up because I was stuck on a word. I can still hear my aunt's voice just like it was yesterday; she would say, "Keep reading," but I couldn't because I did not know the word or would try and skip over the word or I would make up a word.

The class was sectioned off into three areas with different color codes, according to reading abilities. The red was the advance group, the yellow semi-advanced, and the blue was for the intermediate (slow) readers. So, I don't have to say what color group I was assigned to. Every day, as I sat in class, my attention was on the advance group. In my heart, I wanted to be in the advanced reading group. The girls I hung out with were in the advance group, and they would question me about why I was not in their group. This would always make me feel embarrassed.

My teacher never said to the class these were the different reading levels, but every day when it was reading time, we all knew the reading levels were not the same. So the remainder of the day, and every day, I would think to myself, *You are a failure and a dummy.*

Failure and dummy; yes, I said "failure and dummy" because of the crack in my pot. My comprehension was at the lowest level possible. Because of this, when the time came for the quarterly examination in class, I failed. Inside of me, I wanted to pass each examination so badly, but for whatever reason I could not retain the information I had learned. I needed help.

My eight-year-old world was upside down, and I felt ashamed of my learning disability.

So the question at hand was, how could this be? All my friends were leaving me behind. My lifestyle at home was the same. I don't remember any strict instructions about reading or doing homework. Once I got home, I had no assistance in doing my homework, so I did the most of the assignment the best that I could. At home, I did my daily chores of cleaning my mom's house—the bathrooms, the dishes, mopping, and vacuuming the entire house. After doing these chores, I grew to love the chores because when we visited my aunt's house, it was also clean, neat, and in order.

I started to put this into action in my mom's house by keeping it clean and in order as well. I would at least move my mother's furniture around on a weekly basis. I would say to myself, "This is just how I will keep my house when I get grown." So this became the norm for me in keeping my mom's house in order.

Monday through Friday, my duty was cleaning my mom's house. On the weekend, I had to wait until my brothers got out of bed to make their beds. My childhood friends and I made a competition of who had the cleanest apartment in the project where we all lived. As young children, we gave each other tips on how to make the floor shine and the house smelling good. Not to say that my mom would not clean her own home, but mind you, she was working trying to keep food on the table for her four children at the time.

Once I completed the chores, I could go outside to play. I don't remember Mom asking if there was any homework. I didn't know if my mom could help either, because she stopped going to high school in the tenth grade and married my dad; so maybe her reading and comprehension levels were not up to a degree to teach or assist me. But mind you, I had a big brother who was a straight-A student. I don't remember him helping me with my schoolwork either. Most likely he would have helped if I had only asked him.

My big brother was very kind and a quiet person. He never had a lot to say, but must I tell you the pressure of a smart brother? I wanted more than anything to advance in my classes. I always had this question going around and around in my head: "How come I am not as smart as or smarter than my brother and my classmates?" However, this only made the crack in my pot seem more significant.

So the next day at school, I would repeat the same cycle of not reading any better than the day before. Let's not talk about my homework assignment that had to be turned in and graded by my teacher. I remember so clearly each week when my teacher would give us our homework assignments back with the grade posted at the top of the sheet in big bold letters. I was so embarrassed because every time I would have a D or F. Everyone would ask, "What's your grade?"

Why would I want to answer? It was the same as the week before.

At some point throughout the day in my classroom, we had to solve problems on the chalkboard by going to the chalkboard to answer a question. I would pray, *Lord, please don't let my teacher call on me.* But it never failed. I hear my teacher now, "Patricia, go to the board." Being so nervous inside, I could not understand the question the teacher asked me to solve. My insides were telling me, *You're going to answer the question wrong*. No one could see my fear or my thoughts. Fear had a terrible hold on me, to the point of giving up. Sure enough, the answer was wrong, and then the voice would say, *Try it again*.

As the school year ended, I did not graduate to the next grade. Let me back up; during that year, we spent half the school year in Philadelphia, and we soon moved back to Florida, my home state, where I was born and raised.

The report my teacher from Philadelphia sent to my new teacher in Florida said that I needed help in my weak areas of reading, spelling, and pronunciation of words. I will never forget sitting in class thinking, *I will never make it to the next grade because of my inability to read and spell*. Oh, what a cracked pot I was in the Master's hand, shaped for His use.

I remember earlier in the school year the family of one of my classmates was a religious family, so I decided to hang out with her for a few months. The children at school made fun of us. They would talk about the outfits she wore, and they would say things to me like, "Tricia, you know you don't want to be friends with her." She seemed like she could help me with my cracked pot. I was searching for anything that could help me with my failing situation.

So, as I stated earlier, I did not get promoted to the next grade. I was only eight years old. I just could not overcome the shame and embarrassment of not moving forward to the next grade.

After completing two years in the third grade, I was so determined to work hard so that I could make it to the fourth grade the next year. Through the next school year, my mind stayed on repeating a grade. Now I was older than my classmates, and everyone knew I hadn't made it to the next grade.

The school that I attended was a small school, and basically everybody knew each other.

My grades finally started to improve because of the shame and embarrassment. I knew I had to work harder and pay attention more in class. With this in mind, I made it to the next grade.

From that time on, I knew I could not have any distractions from passing my classes. I was determined to move forward to the next grade.

By this time, the school I was attending announced that it would be closing after that school year. Now I was nervous because we would be moving to a larger school with more children. Everyone would know that I had a learning problem. I thought that my failure in spelling and reading would cause me to become the laughingstock of the school. I could feel myself growing weak and thinking I had no hope of getting any better. Was the crack in my pot getting bigger? I knew there was someone greater within me to get this crack in my crackpot together. I could not put my finger on it, but something was happening. Once the school year ended, I told myself, *You must keep it together. School will start back within a couple of months.*

I remember my mother's friend's son was in special education, and I would pray, *Lord, never let me have to go to the special education class.* Due to my inability to comprehend, I knew it could happen to me. The children I grew up with surely didn't mind making fun of me. That was during the start of my elementary school days. As I think over my school days, I really couldn't remember what my greatest subject was. Each day, I said to myself that I would improve, but there was never a time in school where I made an A or a B in my classes.

I remember in one of my classes, I could not pronounce "concert" and "certs." My teacher would tell me to look at the word "concert" and take the "con" off the word. My mind could not do it. Every day, she would have me come to her desk to say these two words. After one year, I finally got them right.

We also had speed-reading in our class; mind you, I did my best to keep up. It was like before I could get the first three words in my mind, the class had already moved into the next paragraph. What a challenge for me! But before I move on, let me interject some words about my granddad.

MY GRANDDAD

I **have talked about my inability of learning and I** would now like to make an insertion about my grandpa, who I called Granddad. He was a godly man who preached the Word of God. As a matter of fact, he ministered the Word of God in a couple of churches, where I knew he was the pastor. He would take my brother and me to church with him; the locations were in my small hometown of Madison, and we also traveled to Quincy, Florida.

I can remember so clearly in my mind when Granddad would tell us to trust the Lord with our whole hearts. I also remember him often telling us the story about Daniel and the three Hebrew boys, whose names were Shadrach, Meshach, and Abednego. I never forgot these Bible stories. My granddad encouraged us in the Lord's word on many occasions; he would often say, "No matter what life situation you may find yourself in, know God is always with you." Yes, with my shortfalls of comprehending, speaking, spelling, and reading, God was the one who was reshaping me for His glory. No matter what I was reading or trying to understand, maybe it was a small word or a gigantic word, God has always seen me through.

Granddad, I thank you for your words of encouragement that have carried me along the way. God's word is exact: Jeremiah 18:4 (NIV) spoke to my heart to write and tell others of my inabilities. Jeremiah says, "But the pot he was shaping from the clay was marred in his hands; so the potter formed it into another pot, shaping it as seemed best to him."

Remembering what my granddad said to me, I soon learned I must keep on keeping on. With my elementary school years behind me, I had to learn I must push forward, and it was going to take hard work. Junior high school was only one summer away, and the butterflies were getting the best of me.

There is more I must say about my granddad. He was a very hard-working man as well. He owned a farm that I can still remember; my oldest brother was born on this particular farm. He was an owner of a small neighborhood store with many homemade baked goods. I know for sure my step-grandmother sold homemade sweet potato pies in one of the stores. The customers would stand in line to get one, and people would make special orders to purchase the sweet potato pies.

My granddad was in charge of several tobacco fields, and I had a job in one of the fields. My position was a lager, and I carried a load of tobacco to the wagon after the primer finished cropping it. The most exciting part was at the end of the day, when I would look at my clothes and see the green stains from carrying the tobacco all day long. Then we would get on the back of Granddad's truck to head home. At the end of each day, we were given our fifty cents. I know you'll say, "WHAT? Fifty cents?"

That was a lot of money back in the early sixties. My brother and I saved our money to help our mother purchase our school clothes.

Not only that, my granddad was a carpenter. I saw him make furniture and sell the items. He made rocking chairs for my mom when she was pregnant with my sister and recliner chairs for my aunt, his daughter. She kept two of the recliners for years, even after Granddad went home to heaven.

My grandmother went home to heaven at the early age of forty. You might have been wondering why I never talked about her; I was too young to remember anything about my grandmother. My aunt told me I was only one month old when she passed away. She also said to me that my grandmother loved me so much, and just before she passed, she told my mother to bring me to her so that she could hold me. I love this part of my life so much. On my mother's side of the family, we are a very close family, and it is a blessing. With the love we have for each other, I wouldn't change this part of the crack in my pot; the situation. More challenges came about in my pot as I moved into the junior high years of my life.

JUNIOR HIGH SCHOOL YEARS

All my disappointments carried into my seventh and eighth grade years. The crack in my pot grew. My grades were never above a C level, and my reading and spelling never changed much. But I did enough to pass to the next class each year after third grade. Little did I know that I would face a new level of pressure and challenges in the coming years. I remember in the seventh and eighth grades, my so-called friends made remarks about my clothes and hygiene. "Her teeth look like butter." "Look at those skinny legs." "Who wants to hang around her? She's ugly." There were many more remarks they made about me daily.

All this would take place as we were walking across the field to catch the school bus back home at the end of each school day. One day I got the courage to tell them I knew they were talking about me. The look on their faces was priceless: *Oh my goodness, she knows what we said*. From that day forward, they did not make any more nasty remarks about me, or at least to my face.

I remember trying out to be a cheerleader and getting rejected because of my grades. I had to maintain a C-grade level in all of my classes to be able to participate in any school activities. My grades were about half and half, with Cs and Ds.

What a big letdown for me. I thought I would have made a great cheerleader. I had the looks. (I was an attractive, young lady, I must say myself.) That was part of the reason I got picked on in school. Now I couldn't find anything I liked to do in school, so I decided to try out for the track team and made it. I soon found out I didn't want to do all that running, so I dropped out. There I go, quitting again. *There, more of the crack in my pot.*

It seemed to me failure was always knocking at my door. There was no one to encourage me. I did not understand the ball was in my court and not in others. My understanding at the time was, *If others can do it, I can too*. However, I did limit myself because I would only go so far, and I would give up and not press forward.

During junior high school years, every girl wanted to look her best. I started focusing my attention on my appearance. Well, I was blessed with the opportunity to go to Miami to spend the summer with my aunt and uncle.

During this stay, my aunt would buy all my school clothes because my mom could not afford them. Therefore, my clothes were lovely, and I would get picked on at school just because of my beautiful clothes and beautiful hair. Mind you, I had lovely hair. My so call friends would make remarks like, "She thinks she looks pretty," and they would pull my hair and tear my clothes. My mom began to tell me, "You better not come home with your hair messed up and your clothes torn." That didn't help in hearing my mother say those words.

I did not know what jealousy was at the time, nor could I spell it. It didn't take long to learn what it meant though. Every day, I was involved in a fight. I could not concentrate on my schoolwork because of what others were doing to me. I was also afraid because my older brother was in high school now.

Remember, I had to repeat the third grade. Yes, I was left without my brother's protection from all my bad schoolmates. The years rolled right along, and I made it to high school. While I was in high school, I decided that I was going to do better, and I also learned to defend myself.

There was a time when exciting things were happening in my life, and part of that was with my family. We had many fun trips to visit my mom's family at my birthplace. The trip would take about thirty minutes at the most and would consist of my mom, my three brothers, my sister and me. As we traveled to our granddad's and aunt's houses, we would listen to a gospel song that was playing on the cassette player in the car. Don't forget, my granddad was a preacher, and my mom was brought up in a Christian home. So, there was nothing like good old gospel music. At the time, some of the songs would bring my mom to tears, and we would all sing along. Sometimes the trip would be for a couple of hours, and other times it would be for a weekend. During our visit, we would have great food to eat, and all the food was homemade. My mom made the best biscuits; I remember many times my mom and her sisters would have conversations, and they would laugh so hard until they cried. I remember when we would all dance and sing songs—songs of Sam Cooke, Otis Redding, Carla Thomas, Betty Wright, and many more. Our granddad—the preacher man—would tell us to turn that music down. We could only go to the movie theater on Saturdays during daylight hours. That was the rule in my granddad's home. No matter what, we all enjoyed the trips.

As the summer ended, and it was time to go back to school, I made it through junior high school and had time to think about moving to high school.

HIGH SCHOOL YEARS

In high school, I had many thoughts about what would happen if I didn't pass these classes. I just might be riding the short yellow bus. No child likes the idea of the short yellow bus. These thoughts motivated me to work hard and pay attention in class.

Yet there were still many more humps and bumps along the way. The crack in my pot was more significant than I could imagine, but with the grace of God and the help of the Lord, I was determined to work harder than ever before.

Along the way, I got sidetracked. I met this young boy, but really, his brother introduced me to him. His brother thought I was an adorable, young lady. The story of this young man... He only came to visit his brother during the summer months. However, this young boy had a girlfriend here in my hometown, but everyone knew she was dating another guy, which is why his brother took it upon himself to introduce him to me. So we met and exchanged phone numbers, and we began to talk on a daily basis. Mind you, he was already finished with high school, and I had just started ninth grade. In one of our conversations, I did let him know if he wanted to date me, he had to ask for my hand in courtship. How many of you are laughing by now? That's the way my mom said it had to be; I could not date anyone unless he asked for my hand in courtship.

The crack in my pot grew worse. Many other things that were not good for me began to unfold in my life. Courtship took my mind off of my schoolwork—the wrong move.

We lived in the projects, and I had this one friend; we would sit on the steps and have conversations about how we wanted our lives to be once we were grown, and what college we would attend when we completed high school.

My school had a job program for seniors to participate in for about two hours a day after school. I signed up and got the job; I think it was because we were a low-income family. I remember those days after school, when I would walk to the city hospital to work as a file clerk. I knew with my reading and spelling ability, I could manage this job. My responsibilities were to put the patient paperwork in the correct files. This job did not take much reading or pronunciation. Matching the name on the paper with the name on the record couldn't be too hard. If the job had required me to apply my reading and spelling, then it would have been more difficult.

After high school, I completed one semester of community college. With my disability of comprehending, my school assignments had failing grades. College was short-term for me. I couldn't keep pretending to my family that I liked college and was making passing grades. The college I attended sent the grades to my mom in the mail. I already knew she was going to find out that I was failing my classes.

Shortly after that, my roommate and friend introduced me to the military through her friend from high school who had gone into the US Army. Listening to her story, I had this thought in my mind: *This might be the right thing for me to do*. My mom and aunt were providing income for me to attend college. The situation: there was a crack in my pot.

LIFE IN THE MILITARY

After thinking this over, enlisting in the army was something I wanted to do. I talked it over with my mom. Her answer was, "If this is something you want to do, this is fine with me." Only a couple of weeks later, my best friend, my friend who told me about the military, and I went downtown to the recruiter station and got the information that we needed to enter the military.

We got scheduled to take the entry test. The day of the test, the three of us passed with flying colors. We entered into the delayed entry program for three-and-a-half months. There was a waiting list for the job we got selected for, which was the reason we were put on the delayed training list.

We went to the airport and within a couple of hours of flying, we all arrived at the MEPS (Military Entrance Processing Station). My best friend, college roommate, and I were now on our way to basic training.

During our physical exam, we all had to get in line and do this thing called "the duck walk," and I am telling you, the only clothes we had on were our underwear. The duck walk required us to squat down and walk forward on our tippy toes; however, it was excruciating for me, and the doctor had me do it twice. I almost didn't make it for basic training because I could not do the duck walk.

The very next day, we got on a plane again and flew to our primary training location. My whole life changed. We got put on a bus that was called a "cattle bus." It took about twenty minutes before we reached our location.

I put my luggage in a building that I found out later was where I would be resting my head for the night. This new location became my home away from home for the next six weeks.

During these six weeks of training, I got very homesick. On the weekends, we were allowed to call home, and every time I called my mom, I would cry and ask her to please come and get me. My mom, my older brother, and my mom's best friend had to calm me down and let me know that everything was going to be okay. I felt that what I was going through would never end. As we processed in the weeks ahead, we got introduced to things this country girl from Florida had never experienced before. I never forgot when we went to the weapon range, I was like, "Oh no." I found out I was a left-hand shooter, due to the fact I could not close my left eye. On my first try at the weapon qualification range, I bowlowed, and my drill sergeant was trying to do everything to get me qualified.

They started yelling at me until I said I couldn't close my eye. I was given an eyepatch to see if that could help. I decided to switch shoulders for the butt of the weapon to rest. Little did I know that I was going to hit all my targets, but in the process, I burned my forearm because I needed a brass reflector. The reflector kept the brass shells from falling on my arms. From that point on, every time I went to the weapon qualification, I was an expert all the way. But in the meantime, we were drilled like nothing before. Anyone who made a mistake had to do push-up after push-up. These mistakes included looking wrong and getting caught, chewing gum, and moving your foot when you were not allowed. The list went on and on. The moment my feet touched the ground, my thoughts were like I had just entered a nightmare. It was non-stop moving and yelling.

I didn't know if I was happy or sad because I had to leave my family. No matter what, I was on my new journey in life with my situation, the crack in my pot. Stay tuned for the continuation of my life in the military.

Jeremiah 18:4 (NIV) – But the pot he was shaping from the clay was marred in his hands; so the potter formed it into another pot, shaping it as seemed best to him.

ABOUT THE AUTHOR

Patricia Ann Dumas Forbes is a native of Madison, Florida. She is a wife and mother of three beautiful children, and a grandmother of ten awesome grandchildren. She works in ministry and is the owner of Royalty Cents, a non-profit business that reaches out to college students and provides hygiene items on a quarterly basis. She is a retired Sergeant First Class from the United States Army, with twenty-two years and twenty-eight days of service. The best is yet to come!

CPSIA information can be obtained
at www.ICGtesting.com
Printed in the USA
LVHW040509050319
609450LV00016B/42